{{code creator}}

T0102015

CODING ACTIVITIES FOR
BUILDING
APPS
WITH PYTHON

Cathleen Small

ROSEN
PUBLISHING

Published in 2022 by The Rosen Publishing Group, Inc.
29 East 21st Street, New York, NY 10010

Library of Congress Cataloging-in-Publication Data

Names: Small, Cathleen, author.
Title: Coding activities for building apps with Python / Cathleen Small.
Description: First edition. | New York : Rosen Publishing, 2022. | Series: Code creator | Audience: Grades 7–12. | Includes bibliographical references and index.
Identifiers: LCCN 2019005868| ISBN 9781725340961 (library bound) | ISBN 9781725340954 (paperback)
Subjects: LCSH: Computer programming—Juvenile literature. | Application software—Development—Juvenile literature. | Python (Computer program language—Juvenile literature.
Classification: LCC QA76.6115 .S628 2022 | DDC 005.1—dc23
LC record available at https://lccn.loc.gov/2019005868

Manufactured in the United States of America

Some of the images in this book illustrate individuals who are models. The depictions do not imply actual situations or events.

CPSIA Compliance Information: Batch #CSRYA22. For further information contact Rosen Publishing, New York, New York at 1-800-237-9932.

Find us on

Contents

Introduction

Who is behind the medical billing systems that hospitals, doctors, and insurance companies use? Coders. What about behind the software used by animators and effects specialists in the film industry? Coders. Who develops *Fortnite*, *Call of Duty*, and other exciting video games? Yes, more coders.

Coding is an exciting and lucrative profession for anyone with an interest in technology or computers. The tech world is constantly changing and expanding, and coding careers are available in nearly every other field, as well. Every industry now uses computer software and applications in one way or another, and it is coders who create that software and those applications.

In the early days of computing, software was king. Anything that was not hardware (the physical pieces of the computer system and its peripherals, such as a keyboard) was software. In a sense, that is still the case: there is hardware (computers, laptops, tablets, smartphones, printers, and so on), and then there are the software programs that run on them. However, recent years of computing have seen the rise of one specific type of software: the application, better known as an app.

Applications are pieces of software that are executable. That is, they run and perform an activity or set of tasks on their own. All applications are executable, and all applications are software— but not every piece of software is an application; software that is not executable is not generally considered an app.

Most of the software people use is for the purpose of doing something (a task or set of tasks), so much of what people use today is applications. Accordingly, coding for apps is an in-demand field with many opportunities.

The opportunities are limitless when it comes to coding, with new apps being developed every day by both experienced professionals and enthusiastic amateurs.

Apps can be written in many different programming languages, and everyone has their favorites. Some frequently used programming languages for building apps include: Java, JavaScript, PHP, C++, Objective-C, C#, Perl, and HTML. The platform the app is intended for (i.e., MacOS, iOS, Windows, or Android) sometimes determines the best programming language to use, but some languages can be used to develop apps for multiple platforms. For example, Swift was

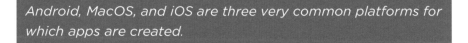

Android, MacOS, and iOS are three very common platforms for which apps are created.

created by Apple and is used for creating apps for MacOS and iOS, while Perl is generally used for developing Android apps.

One of the most commonly used programming languages for multiplatform development is Python. It is relatively simple and very versatile, making it a good first language for aspiring coders. It is also considered a strong general-purpose programming language, meaning it can be used for nearly any type of programming. It can run on

Python is a solid choice as a first programming language for new coders. It is simple and incredibly versatile.

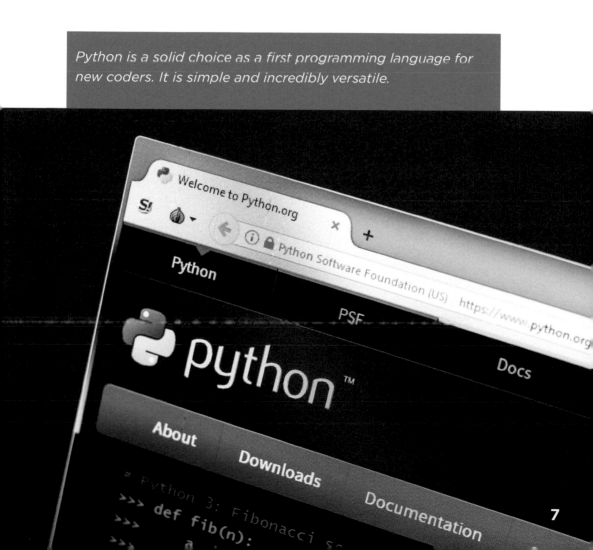

multiple platforms, including Windows, MacOS, Linux, and Unix. To give an idea of just how widely used Python is: it is the language behind Google's search engine, YouTube, and the New York Stock Exchange's web transaction system.

Because Python is so versatile and very readable, all of the code blocks in this book will use Python. You will learn to use Python to do simple math, work with strings, compare and convert data, store variables, send email, and even create a few simple games.

Though it may seem scary, do not be daunted by learning a new language. By starting to code in small snippets, you will build a strong foundation for future learning. After you have learned to create these pieces of applications, you will be well equipped to explore application programming on a larger scale—using Python or branching out to another language.

Ready to jump in and start learning Python to build apps? There are a few ways to get started. You can download the latest version of Python from https://python.org and open the command line on your computer. How you access the command line depends on your operating system, but a quick internet search should tell you how to do it on your machine. Alternatively, you can use text-editing software, such as Text Editor for Windows or TextEdit for Mac. Finally, you can use an integrated development environment (IDE) to write your code.

There are a number of free IDEs you can download and use to practice your coding. For Python, PyCharm is particularly user-friendly. All of the code for this book was developed and tested in PyCharm. It would be impossible to give instructions for how to use every IDE out there, but if you choose to download PyCharm, here are some general instructions for downloading, launching, and using it:

- Run a search for PyCharm on the website to access the latest version for your operating system.
- Download it and install PyCharm in the desired location on your computer.
- When you first launch the app, you will see a welcome window with a few options; creating a new project will allow you to name a new project (whatever you like) and launch it in the PyCharm virtual environment.

PyCharm is a robust IDE that allows you to do many things, but when you are just playing with code and testing it, scratch files are an easy way to go. In the file menu, right-click and follow "New>New Scratch File." A submenu will show up in the middle of the IDE, from which you can select "Python." A blank scratch file will open.

You can play in this scratch file to your heart's content. When you are ready to try running a script, either right-click again and select "run," or press the green play arrow at the top of the window. Doing either will open a pane at the bottom of the screen, where you will see the output of your program.

If you get stuck with PyCharm itself, the help menu can guide you through the application. If you get stuck on your script, PyCharm will try to guide you with tips about what line in your script is problematic. If you are still stuck, try searching the internet. There are Python user forums with answers to many, many common issues. Ready to go? Time to get started!

Activity 1

Hello, World! Getting Your Feet Wet with Python

"Hello, World!" is the first program nearly everyone starts out with when learning to code. Is it exciting? Not terribly. Is it easy and useful? Yes, depending on the language you are using. In Java, printing "Hello, World!" requires this syntax:

```
public class MyHelloWorldProgram {
    public status void main(String []args) {
        System.out.println("Hello, World!");
    }
}
```

That seems like a lot of unnecessary work. We can try that again in Python. Fire up your IDE or text editor and type the following syntax:

```
print("Hello, World!")
```

That is all it takes. If you are using PyCharm, press the green right-facing arrow to run your script.

Things are a little more complex if you are using text-editing software. Type your syntax, as above, and then save the file as HelloWorld.py. This is called saving a script. Next, go to the command line—make sure you are in the directory where your script is saved (you can use the "cd" command to change your directory)—and type the following line to execute the script you just saved:

python HelloWorld.py

Your output of "Hello, World!" should display at the command line. Congratulations on creating your first Python program! It may not be very exciting, but it is still a fully functioning program.

If you are printing text on a screen as part of a larger application, you are likely to be printing more than just one line of text. For example, what if you want to print a person's name and contact information? Try it now: type "print" and a name and address, hitting the return key between each line of the contact info, as it would appear on the front of a letter. What happens when you run the program?

You likely got a syntax error—something along the lines of this:

SyntaxError: EOL while scanning string literal

enclose the string in quotes. For example, if you wanted to build a game app that greets players by saying "Happy" and the day of the week, you could define variable strings for each day of the week, like this:

```
monday_closing = "Happy Monday!"
tuesday_closing = "Happy Tuesday!"
wednesday_closing = "Happy Wednesday!"
```

Follow this formula for all seven days of the week. Then, in the app, you could include the Python script:

```
print(monday_closing)
```

That would be a bit of a pain, though. It would be just as easy to type this, right?

```
print("Happy Monday!")
```

If you did that, however, you would need to change the message for each day of the week, because you would not want to say "Happy Monday!" on a Friday.

Think big. Python is flexible and allows you to do pretty much anything you want. If you can code it, you can do it. As you learn more about coding in Python, you could easily build a short if-else structure (more on that later) into your app that checks the day of the week and then prints the appropriate string accordingly.

A little tip about strings: They can contain letters, numbers, or characters, but certain characters can cause a problem. Apostrophes and quote marks, for example. Suppose you coded this into your app:

print("They call me the "Game Master."")

That includes two sets of quotes, which is a problem. Python will not know what to do with this, and you will wind up with an error. There is a simple fix, though. You simply include a "\" before the troublesome character. Change the statement to this:

print("They call me the \"Game Master.\"")

Now Python will print:

They call me the "Game Master."

Crisis averted, just like that.

Activity 3

What Date Is It?

Maybe you want to alert users of the date and time when they log on. Like most things in Python, this is a simple process. In fact, Python includes a simple library feature called datetime. At the beginning of your Python script to retrieve the date and time, you can call the datetime library:

from datetime import datetime

Now you have the library, you just need to print it for users. The print command comes into play again:

print(datetime.now())

Why the ".now()"? Remember that datetime is an entire library. If you just use this syntax:

print(datetime)

You will not get the date and time—you will get a cryptic message. Adding .now() tells the script that you want to print the current date and time from the datetime library. It prints in a strange format, though. If you are working along with this activity, you no doubt saw an output that looks like this:

2019-12-25 19:45:31.221489

That is a date and time, all right, but not a usable one. To print the date in a more user-friendly style, assign a variable to the current date and time retrieved from the datetime library. Your script should look like this:

```
from datetime import datetime
current_daytime = datetime.now()
```

This short script tells Python that every time you type "current_daytime," you want the time it currently is. Now you can play around with that variable and extract the month, day, and year from it. Python has specific commands to do so. Add the following to your script:

```
print(current_daytime.month)
print(current_daytime.day)
print(current_daytime.year)
```

That is still going to print your date in a poor format:

12
25
2019

Now, however, you can use your knowledge of printing constant strings to make this look a lot better. You just need to know two more bits of info. The first is how to turn integers into strings. The output returned for the date is returned in the form of integers, but it should be put into a nice string sentence. You cannot combine integers with strings in a print statement, but you can turn integers into strings using the str() function. For example, "str(current_daytime.month)" will turn the integer for the month into a string that can then be printed with other strings.

The second piece of info you need is how to concatenate strings—in other words, how to add them together. You simply use a "+" symbol to add them together. For example, you could print "Hi there" by using this syntax:

print("Hi there")

That makes sense—but you could also use this syntax:

print("Hi " + "there")

Normally, the first syntax is cleaner and easier, but if you are trying to combine multiple data types, the second syntax becomes necessary. Note also that spaces need to be inside the quote marks (either after the first word or before the second), or they will not print. This:

print("Hi" + "there")

Will result in this:

Hithere

Anyway, back to the date. Try to print the current date in a readable format using this:

print("It is " + str(current_daytime.month) + "/"
  + str(current_daytime.day) + "/" + str(current_
  daytime.year) + ". Welcome!")

Your output should look like this:

It is 12/25/2019. Welcome!

Notice that there is a space after the word "is" in the syntax, so we make sure there is a space before the date. Also notice that the forward slashes typically used in standard date format (at least in the United States) are included in quote marks because they are strings—and they have no spaces around them because dates do not usually have spaces around the slashes. Finally, notice that the final string starts with a period and a space. By doing this, Python knows to put a period after the date, add a space, and then include the final statement: "Welcome!"

Not so hard, right? To do the same thing with the time, Python lets you extract and use that data with the syntax hour, minute, and second.

Activity 4

You Do the Math

One thing computers and applications are really good at is math. People make mistakes in math, but computer programs and applications never do. Most apps require—at the very least—some sort of arithmetic computations. Some even require advanced math. Think of an app for a small online boutique or store: it will have to perform simple math to add up the value of items in a user's shopping cart, calculate tax and shipping costs, and provide the user with a grand total. Games that use a token or other monetary system to allow players to "buy" items similarly have to perform basic computations. An app that computes returns on investments will obviously have to perform more complicated calculations. No matter the complexity of the math, the application can handle it as long as the coder writes the program correctly.

Do a little math to calculate revenue from a yard sale. Suppose a neighbor was having a yard sale and said he had a spare table you could use to sell a few items. You decided to sell some old books you have already read. Assume that you price children's books at $1 each, young adult fiction books at $2 each, trade paperbacks at $3 each, and new-release hardcovers at $5 each. Also assume you have ten of each type of book on the table, for a total of forty books. The neighbor is handling all the cash at the sale and tells you that you should calculate your earnings at the end of the day, and he will give you that amount.

At the end of the day, you realize you sold all ten children's books, nine young adult fiction books, eight trade paperbacks, and seven new-release hardbacks. You could calculate your proceeds out on paper or in your head, but it would be so much more fun to write a little Python script to do it for you.

First, you need to define a variable, which is a value that can change over time. In Python, it is quick and easy to define a variable. In this case, you will want to define a variable to hold the result for the number of each type of book sold times the price, like this:

childrens_books_sold = 10 * 1

Ten is the number of children's books you sold, and they sold for $1 each. In Python, the asterisk (*) is the multiplication operator. Note that the variable very specifically defines what the value describes. You can use almost anything you want for a variable name. You could easily type:

```
x = 10 * 1
```

instead of:

childrens_books_sold = 10 * 1

However, "x" is not very descriptive for anyone else looking at your app. Or, you might revisit your app a year or two in the future and have no idea what "x" was supposed to define. In contrast, if you go back a year or two later and see a variable called "childrens_books_sold," it is pretty obvious what it is defining. It may take a little longer to type out the longer variable, but it will likely save you some confusion in the future.

Continue on for the rest of the types of books:

young_adult_books_sold = 9 * 2
trade_paperbacks_sold = 8 * 3
hardbacks_sold = 7 * 5

Now you have the total for each type of book sold—but you want a grand total. Add all of your variables together and assign them to another new variable:

```
total_sold = childrens_books_sold + young_
  adult_books_sold + trade_paperbacks_sold +
  hardbacks_sold
```

Now all you have to do is print the value of "total_sold" to the screen:

```
print(total_sold)
```

Notice that there are no quote marks around total_sold. That's because it is a variable—not a string. If you put quotes around it, the program will print:

```
total_sold
```

instead of the actual number:

```
87
```

Obviously, 87 is the value you want—that is how much money you need to collect for selling your books.

Alongside "+" for addition and "*" for multiplication, Python uses a "-" for subtraction, a "/" for division, and a "%" for division with a remainder. If you use "/" instead of "%" for a division problem where the result is not a whole number, the result will be rounded down. So "9 / 2" would return a product of "4" instead of 4.5. In contrast, "9 % 2" would produce "1," because "1" is the remainder after the division operation. The usual order of operations applies when calculating in Python: parentheses, exponents, multiplication, division, addition, and subtraction.

Activity 5

Booleans: Fun to Say and Fun to Use!

Now that you've done a little work with variables, it is time to meet a special type of variable: the Boolean. "Boolean" is a fancy word that simply describes a value that can be either true or false—but nothing in between. Booleans are used fairly often in programming. One example would be a website that requires a user to be a certain age. Social media sites often ask for users' birthdates to determine whether they are thirteen years or older. If they are not yet thirteen years old, they cannot use the site.

For a simple example of Booleans in action, think about the yard sale discussed earlier. Suppose your neighbor told you that if your total sold was at least $50, he would match your earnings. In your head, you know that $87 is more than $50, so your neighbor will be matching your earnings. You could write a simple addition operation to multiply $87 by two and determine the total amount your neighbor owes you. Or, you could have more fun and work with a Boolean.

For starters, you will need to define a new variable below your "total_sold:"

total_sold_plus_match = total_sold * 2

Now to add in the Boolean. Just like in regular math notation, the ">" symbol indicates greater-than and the "<" symbol indicates less-than. You need to determine if your total sold is greater than $50, and in Python, you do that by using an if statement.

if total_sold > 50:
    print(total_sold_plus_match)

If that looks a little confusing, keep reading. In Python, you can comment on your code by using a "#" at the beginning of a line. In programming, comments are short explanations of what is happening in the code. Comments are used to help your code be readable to other coders (and to you, if you go back and look at it long after you have moved on to bigger and better programs). Python does not execute any statements that begin with a "#" symbol. Look at that last block of code again:

```
#Need to define how much our neighbor owes us if
   they match our earnings
total_sold_plus_match = total_sold * 2
#Need to determine whether the total_sold is
   greater than 50
if total_sold > 50:
    #If it is, then we can print the new total to show
       our neighbor
    print(total_sold_plus_match)
```

Make sense? Like creating descriptive variables, commenting code takes some time, but it pays off in the end when your code is readable and easy to use or debug as needed. There is one more thing to do to this code, though. What if your neighbor had agreed to match your earnings only if they were greater than $100? You sold $87, so what would the output be? Change the 50 to 100:

```
if total_sold > 100:
    print(total_sold_plus_match)
```

With that code, you can see that it just returns 87 by default. That is correct—you did not break $100, so your neighbor owes you $87. However, it would be more accurate (and better coding) to tell the app what to do if you do not meet the threshold of your if statement. You can do that by adding an else statement:

```
if total_sold > 100:
    print(total_sold_plus_match)
#Tell the program to just return total_sold if the
  100 threshold is not met
else: print(total_sold)
```

An else statement is simple, but it performs an important task. If statements describe what the program should do if something is true; an else statement describes what the program should do if it is false. In this book sale example, the if statement just tells the program what to do when the "total_sold" is more than 100. The else statement is instructing the program on how to act when the "total_sold" is *not* more than 100. Now the app knows exactly what to do: if 100 is met, the "total_sold" is multiplied by two and the result is printed to the screen. If the 100 is not met, "total_sold" is printed to the screen without being doubled.

Take a moment, now, to look at the indentation in this final code snippet. The first and fourth lines of this block are both are left-aligned. The second line of code, however, is indented. That spacing is used to indicate that the indented line is related to the left-aligned statement above it. If you sold more than $100, then the short code block in the following two lines should execute. If you did not, then the program just skips the indented code lines and goes right to the final line of code in the snippet (the else statement), which is not indented. Indenting blocks of code is a programming convention, and Python will return an indentation error if it thinks you have indented incorrectly.

Activity 6

Let the User Have a Turn!

It is always useful to know how to use strings, integers, variables, constants, and Booleans, but eventually you will want to branch out and build an app that allows user interaction. To do that, you need to learn how to collect and use input from users of your app.

If you want users to enter data, you can use the raw_input() function. Remember the str() function that turned integers or other data into strings? Similarly, raw_input() is simply a function that prompts the user for input and accepts it. Suppose you are building an app for which you would like to collect some basic user info, such as a name and an email address. You can use raw_input() to do that and create variables to store that information. You need variables because this input will change based on the user who is entering the information.

```
first_name = raw_input("Enter your first name: ")
last_name = raw_input("Enter your last name: ")
email = raw_input("Enter your email address: ")
```

There are a couple of things to notice here. Prompting the user for first and last name separately will allow you to store that data in two separate variables. That may be useful if you wish to address the user in your app at some point. Also note the space after the colon in each line, before the closing quote mark. That is for aesthetics. Without it, the user input would look like this:

Enter your first name:John
Enter your last name:Doe
Enter your email address:JohnDoe@email.com

There is not really anything wrong with that, but it does not look very nice. Adding the space solves the issue. Now you can use the data you have collected to reply to the user:

print("Thank you for joining us, " + str(first_name)
+ ". If we need to reach you, we will email you at "
+ str(email))

Do not forget to use the str() function to convert that user input into strings if you want to print it back with other string data.

To test your first user-driven program, locate the directory in which your scratch file is located and right-click on the scratch file with this code block.

Activity 7

Conversion Challenge

You want to open the file using a program called Python Launcher, which should have come bundled with Python when you originally downloaded it. Now that you know how to do math in Python and how to query users for input, one fun challenge is to build an automatic converter. Of course, such tools already exist on the internet, but it is much more fun to build your own. Why not, when it is this easy?

Begin with a tool that converts the temperature in Fahrenheit to the temperature in Celsius. In the United States, Fahrenheit is the standard for temperature. To convert the temperature in Fahrenheit to Celsius (which many other countries use), simply subtract 32 degrees from the temperature and multiply by 5/9. Start by asking the user for the temperature in Fahrenheit:

```
fahrenheit = int(raw_input("Please enter the
   temperature in degrees Fahrenheit: "))
```

The int() function here is to designate the user's input as an integer—not a string. Normally, user input is in the form of strings, but to perform a mathematical operation, the input must be designated as an integer. In the second line of the script, perform the calculation:

celsius = (fahrenheit - 32) * 5 / 9

Now you can print the result:

```
print("The temperature in Fahrenheit is " +
    str(fahrenheit) + ", and the temperature in Celsius
    is " + str(celsius))
```

Pretty easy. To flip it around to see the temperature—in Fahrenheit—of all those other countries that use Celsius, just flip the script, more or less:

```
celsius = int(raw_input("Please enter the
    temperature in degrees Celsius: "))
fahrenheit = ((9 * celsius) / 5) + 32
print("The temperature in Celsius is " + str(celsius)
    + ", and the temperature in Fahrenheit is " +
    str(fahrenheit))
```

Want to try one more conversion just for fun? How about miles to kilometers, since the United States is one of the few countries to use miles instead of kilometers to measure distance.

The general structure of the conversion program looks similar; only the equation really changes:

```
miles = float(raw_input("Enter the number of
  miles: "))
km = 1.609 * miles
print("A distance of " + str(miles) + " miles is equal
  to " + str(km) + " kilometers.")
```

Notice the use of the float() function in the first line. A float is a real number that may have decimal places—as opposed to using an int() function to return an integer, which has no decimal places. Conversions are so simple to do that you could easily build many different types into one script. An idea for your next app, perhaps?

Activity 8

Fun with Functions

You have seen functions already, even if you did not realize it. A function is simply a named segment of code that performs some sort of task. Python has a number of built-in functions, and you can also import modules into your code that contain additional functions.

Back in Activity 3, you used the str() function to turn data into a string. In Activity 6, you used the raw_input() function to collect user input. Take a look at some other functions built into Python.

The function len() will return the length of a string. A code snippet using this function might look like this:

```
#Collect the name and print it if it is more than five
    characters or return the length if it is less than
    five characters
name = raw_input("What is your name? ")
if len(name) > 5:
    print(len(name))
else:
    print(name)
```

The functions .upper() and .lower() will return a string in all capital letters or all lowercase, respectively. These functions get added to the end of the variable in a statement. To the block of code, add the following two lines (not indented, as they are not part of the if-else structure).

```
print(name.upper())
print(name.lower())
```

If you run the script again, it should ask for a name. If the name is greater than five characters, the output will look something like this:

```
8
CATHLEEN
cathleen
```

If the name is fewer than five characters, the output will look something like this:

```
Ann
ANN
ann
```

If you need to find the minimum or the maximum number in a set of arguments, you can use the min()

and max() functions, respectively. For example, you might build a gaming app that keeps track of users' scores. To find the highest score out of all users, you could designate the users' scores as the arguments in the max() function, like this:

maximum = max(12550, 8000, 14125, 0, 18040)
print("The highest score is " + str(maximum))

There are many other functions you can use in Python, but that gives you a sampling of a few of the more common ones you may need when building apps.

Activity 9

Let's Roll the Dice

Want to have a little fun? How about building a simple dice game? Games are fun, but they are also a great way to learn—especially in Python. Even if you have no intention of building games with your newfound programming knowledge, the skills you learn while building the next few games can easily translate to other types of apps you might want to build.

The dice game you will develop uses a function called randint() that is not included in Python. That means it needs to be imported. You can import entire modules, but they are very big. They contain many functions—the one you need, as well as many you probably do not need. In the interest of keeping your apps running quickly and smoothly, it is best to import only the functions you need, rather than the entire module. To import the randint() function from the random module, type this:

from random import randint

While you are at it, import one more function—the sleep() function from the time module. The sleep() function pauses script execution for a designated amount of time, measured in seconds, so that the processes in the script do not all execute instantly. You want to simulate the rolling of dice, after all, and that takes a few seconds.

```
from time import sleep
```

Now you can simulate the rolling of a pair of dice. To keep this a little more interesting, have the computer roll the dice three times and print out all three rolls. First, let the user know what the game is all about:

```
print("It is time to roll the dice three times and see
    which roll is the highest! Are you ready?")
```

Then, define a function called roll_dice() using def. The roll_dice() function takes an argument of the total number possible from a roll, which is 12 (given that each die has a maximum value of 6 and there are two dice). The code below is commented for explanatory purposes:

```
def roll_dice(number_of_sides):
#For each roll, randint takes arguments of a
    minimum value of 2 and a maximum value of
    number_of_sides because no roll can be less than 1
        first_roll = randint(2,number_of_sides)
        second_roll = randint(2,number_of_sides)
        third_roll = randint(2,number_of_sides)
```

```
#The sleep function takes a number of seconds as
   its argument
      sleep(2)
#After two seconds of sleep, print the result
   of the roll
      print("The first roll is " + str(first_roll))
      sleep(2)
      print("The second roll is " + str(second_roll))
      sleep(2)
      print("The third roll is " + str(third_roll))
```

You defined the function above and now you can call the function to launch the program. Be sure to include the maximum value of 12 as an argument here:

roll_dice(12)

After the function has finished, print a thank you message to the player:

print("Thanks for playing!")

There is a lot going on here, but it should all look fairly familiar. This is not exactly the most exciting game ever written, but using your imagination, you can come up with a lot of fun ways to use the randint function for games! Just make sure you import it in each program.

Activity 10

Take a Guess

Another fun way to use a randomizer is in a guessing game, where the user has to guess what number the computer is "thinking." The overall structure is similar to the dice-rolling game, but this game can allow for more user interaction. When building game apps, user interaction is key!

To get started, import the randint() function and the sleep() function:

from random import randint
from time import sleep

Remember that randint() can take arguments to set some limits, so do that here. Make the number range 1 to 100.

number = randint(1,100)

You could let the user have an infinite number of chances to guess the number, but that would get rather tedious. Instead, set the number of guesses to a maximum of seven. This can be accomplished by initializing the variable guesses at 0 and then setting a while loop.

```
guesses = 0
print("You have a total of seven chances to guess
   the computer\'s number. Let\'s begin.")
while guesses < 7:
    guess = int(raw_input("Please guess a number
       between 1 and 100: "))
    guesses += 1
    print("This is guess number " + str(guesses))
```

There is some new syntax in the previous code block, as well as some bits that might need a quick review. Most importantly, the while loop: a while loop directs a program to execute repeatedly until the condition is no longer true (or, *while* a condition is true). In this case, the condition is that the user must not have gone over seven guesses. The next new bit is the line:

guesses += 1

This is a way to iterate the "guesses" variable and keep track of how many times the user has guessed. The syntax "+= 1" adds one to the current value of the variable "guesses," which will count up toward seven. The last line prints for the user what guess number they are on so they can keep track of their own progress.

Continuing the code block (and still within the while loop, so watch the indentation), create the response to the user's guess:

```
if guess < number:
    print("Your guess is too low.")
elif guess > number:
    print("Your guess is too high.")
else:
    print("You guessed it in " + str(guesses) +
"! Congratulations!")
    sleep(2)
    break
print("The program will now exit.")
```

Note that you don't need any code to end the while loop. In an if-else loop, the else kind of sets the end of the loop. A while loop does not need an end because the parameter is already set: *"while a condition is true, do this process."* When the condition is no longer true, the script knows to exit the while loop.

Also notice that the final print() statement occurs outside of the while loop. That is important, because otherwise the program will print that it is going to exit on every iteration through the loop.

Also note the "elif" in the snippet above. That is Python shorthand for else-if. It is basically the middle part of the if-else loop: *if* A is true, do X; *else if* B is true, do Y; *else*, do Z. These loops can have more than one elif, too, which helps separate them from the Booleans discussed earlier. If there are multiple conditions (more than just true or false), using an else-if loop is your best bet.

Remember the sleep() function from earlier? It has returned here, just to give the user a few seconds to read the results of their final guess before being presented with a statement that the program will now exit. It is not a required part of the script, but it does make the output a little easier for users to follow, so it is a nice touch. That's it—a simple guessing game, created in just a few lines of Python code.

Career Connections

These activities have taught the basics of coding in Python. Python is a great base language to learn because it is fairly simple and it can be used to quickly create and test short scripts to learn new coding concepts. In addition, Python comes with a large standard library of functions to use, such as print(), str(), raw_input(), and more. Importing additional libraries is simple, giving users access to further functionality with little extra code.

Once you have learned Python, you are well on the path to building your career in coding.

```java
/**
 * Handling the operation.
 * @param key pressed operator's key.
 */
public void handleOperator(String key) {
    if (operator.equals("+"))
        number += Double.valueOf(display.getText());
    else if (operator.equals("-"))
        number -= Double.valueOf(display.getText());
    else if (operator.equals("*"))
        number *= Double.valueOf(display.getText());
    else if (operator.equals("/"))
        number /= Double.valueOf(display.getText());
    else if (operator.equals("="))
        number = Double.valueOf(display.getText());
    display.setText(String.valueOf(number));
    operator = key;
    isFirstDigit = true;
}
```

```java
public static void main(String[] args) {
```

Many of the concepts covered here are applicable in other programming languages as well. Loops and functions exist in pretty much every programming language, so learning the basics of how to use them will provide a good foundation for learning how to perform tasks in other coding environments.

The scripts written in this book were simple, but the skills learned from them can be applied to more complex, functional scripts and to eventually coding full-fledged apps. For example, printing "Hello, World!" is easy and relatively pointless—minus the fun factor—but virtually any app you design will require print functions, so knowing how to use the print() function in Python, even in the simplest of scripts, creates a building block. You built on the very first building block by learning how to print values from variables and how to concatenate strings to print more complex statements.

The same is true for all of the skills covered in this book. Learn them at their simplest, but then go back and look at them and think of how you could build them into something much more elaborate and useful. The simple dice-rolling game? Probably as pointless as "Hello, World!," but the value of knowing how to implement a randomizer is undeniable. Some fairly successful applications are built around randomizers. Think of Elfster, a website that allows users to create "secret Santa" types of gift exchanges. At its core, Elfster is a randomizer program. However, that simple function created a website that filled a niche in the industry, and the people behind Elfster have reaped the benefits in profits.

Python is a great language to start with, and spending a long time refining your coding skills by learning how to do more within it is time well spent. Many seasoned programmers use Python on a daily basis. Additionally, Python serves as a great starting point to learn more languages. The basic logic in Python will transfer easily to other languages you might want to learn.

Why bother learning other languages if you become a Python master? Two words: career options. As you refine your coding interests and start thinking about what you would like to pursue a career in, you can research what languages are typically used to program apps in that field. For example, aspiring game programmers will likely want to learn Java, C++, C#, or Objective-C, depending on what platform they want to develop games for. The same is generally true for people wanting to code for virtual reality development, with the addition of JavaScript. Someone wanting to build ecommerce apps is likely to want to learn PHP, which is one of the most widely used languages among developers of ecommerce sites.

For aspiring game coders, Java is a good choice for a next language to learn. It is both popular and well established.

In other words, Python will serve you well—and can also be considered a gateway to other languages. Appreciate the versatility and simplicity of Python, and also appreciate it as a building block to a future in computer science.

If your career interests lie in coding apps, you are in luck—the field of app development is wide open. Thousands of new apps are developed every day. Some are brand-new concepts, and others are unique spins on existing ideas. There is room for everyone. Amazon may have cornered the market on online shopping sites, but it is far from the only one—ecommerce websites pop up all the time, typically handling a specific niche in the market. Just because Amazon is the biggest player does not mean no one else can participate.

If you have a new idea, it can be all the more exciting! Think about Uber, for example. Before early 2009, Uber did not exist. If people needed a ride, they summoned a taxi or called a friend for a lift. Then Uber came along and the face of transportation changed drastically—all because of an app for a new service. Maybe you do not have a new idea and you are not a risk-taker. Maybe you just like coding but you want to do it with the relative security of a full-time job. There is boundless opportunity there, too. Major tech companies are always hiring coders, as are smaller startups. There is no shortage of job opportunities for skilled and interested coders.

One of the beauties of coding is that it can be a largely self-taught skill. Earning a college degree in computer science will open many doors—you will likely have your pick of jobs in any segment of the coding industry if you get a degree and demonstrate proficiency in coding with at least a

Taking a class is an excellent way to sharpen your coding skills, but you can also teach yourself how to code by working through online tutorials or reading programming books.

few popular programming languages. However, you do not have to wait for college to start developing your skills—you can teach yourself coding through books, through online classes and tutorials, and through courses offered at school or through local community colleges.

The same holds true if college is not in your future. College can open many doors, but if you are unable to attend, your dream of having a career in coding lives on. Some companies are willing to hire skilled coders who do not have a degree. The pay may not be as high and you may not have as many immediate options as those with a degree, but there are options. More than anything, it is important that you understand whatever coding languages are needed in the fields you are interested in. If you have talent and drive—along with a lot of programming experience—a college degree is just a cherry on top. So start with Python, try these simple app activities, and then let the sky be the limit.

Glossary

Android A major mobile operating system developed by Google.

argument A value passed to a function in a computer program.

command line A means of interacting with a computer program without going through a graphical user interface.

concatenate To link together in a series.

constant A value that does not change.

integer A whole number.

integrated development environment (IDE) A software application that commonly includes a source code editor, build-automation tools, and a debugging feature and allows coders to develop software more easily.

iOS A major mobile operating system developed by Apple.

Linux A free operating system developed for computers in the early 1990s.

MacOS An operating system for desktop and laptop computers developed by Apple.

niche A specialized segment of a market.

peripheral A device that can be attached to or used with a computer but is not a part of the computer hardware itself.

platform The operating system, hardware, or web browser where a particular software program is executed.

script A series of instructions that are to be carried out in a specific order.

search engine A program that performs searches of the World Wide Web.

string A sequence of letters, characters, or words.

syntax The arrangement of terms and rules that make up a language.

Unix An operating system for computers, first developed in the 1960s.

variable A piece of data that can take on more than one value during the running of a computer program or script.

Windows An operating system for computers and laptops, created by Microsoft in the 1980s.

For More Information

Canada Learning Code
129 Spadina Avenue
Toronto, ON M5V 2L3
Canada
Website: www.canadalearningcode.ca
Facebook: @CanadaLearningCode
Instagram and Twitter: @learningcode
Canada Learning Code is dedicated to ensuring that
    all Canadians have the chance to learn coding skills
    to empower themselves for a future tech career or
    simply to flourish in the digital world.

CanCode
C. D. Howe Building
235 Queen Street, 1st Floor, West Tower
Ottawa, ON K1A 0H5
Canada
1-800-328-6189
Website: https://www.ic.gc.ca/eic/site/121.nsf
    /eng/home
Sponsored by the government of Canada, the
    CanCode program is an outreach and funding
    organization dedicated to increasing computer
    literacy across the country. Its website offers
    a brief introduction to its mission and other
    programs it has funded.

Codecademy
575 Broadway, 5th floor
New York, NY 10012
Website: www.codecademy.com
Facebook and Twitter: @Codecademy
Codecademy is an online educational experience
where users are empowered to learn to code
through online tutorials that range from simple to
challenging. The robust Codecademy community is
a great place to find answers to coding questions.

Code Wizards HQ
13740 Research Boulevard, Building N, Suite 2B
Austin, TX 78750
(800) 213-2417
Website: www.codewizardshq.com
Facebook and Twitter: @CodeWizardsHQ
Code Wizards HQ is an online learning program where
students attend virtual classes led by instructors
who are available in real-time for questions.
Students complete a capstone project at the end
of each twelve-week course and earn a certificate
of completion.

Digital Media Academy
105 Cooper Court
Los Gatos, CA 95032
(866) 656-3342
Website: www.digitalmediaacademy.org

Facebook: @digitalmediaacademy.org
Instagram: @digitalmediaacademy
Twitter: @DMA_org
Digital Media Academy offers tech camps for kids and teens across the United States and in Canada.

Girls Who Code
28 West 23rd Street, 4th Floor
New York, NY 10010
Website: www.girlswhocode.com
Facebook, Instagram, and Twitter: @GirlsWhoCode
Girls Who Code seeks to close the gender gap in the technology field and empower females to pursue careers in computer science and related fields. It offers programs in the United States and Canada, with plans to further expand in the future.

Tynker
280 Hope Street
Mountain View, CA 94041
Website: www.tynker.com
Facebook and Twitter: @GoTynker
Instagram: @tynkercoding
Tynker is an online coding platform for kids. The visual nature of Tynker makes it appealing for the youngest aspiring coders, but older kids who are just starting out may find its user-friendly environment a good place to start building skills.

For Further Reading

Benedict, Aaron, and David Gallaher. *Using Computer Science in High-Tech Health and Wellness Careers.* New York, NY: Rosen Publishing, 2017.

Gonzales, Andrea, and Sophie Houser. *Girl Code: Gaming, Going Viral, and Getting It Done.* New York, NY: Harper Collins, 2017.

Hand, Carol. *Using Computer Science in High-Tech Criminal Justice Careers.* New York, NY: Rosen Publishing, 2017.

Marji, Majed. *Learn to Program with Scratch: A Visual Introduction to Programming with Games, Art, Science, and Math.* San Francisco, CA: No Starch Press, 2014.

Matthes, Eric. *Python Crash Course: A Hands-On, Project-Based Introduction to Programming.* San Francisco, CA: No Starch Press, 2015.

Moritz, Jeremy. *Code for Teens: The Awesome Beginner's Guide to Programming.* Herndon, VA: Mascot Books, 2018.

Niver, Heather Moore. *Careers for Tech Girls in Computer Science.* New York, NY: Rosen Publishing, 2015.

Staley, Erin. *Career Building Through Creating Mobile Apps.* New York, NY: Rosen Publishing, 2014.

Strom, Chris. *3D Game Programming for Kids: Create Interactive Worlds with JavaScript.* Raleigh, NC: Pragmatic Bookshelf, 2018.

Vaidyanathan, Sheena. *Creative Coding in Python: 30+ Programing Projects in Art, Games, and More.* Beverly, MA: Quarry Books, 2018.

Bibliography

Bradford, Laurence. "Python 2 vs. Python 3: Which Should I Learn?" Learn to Code with Me, August 8, 2018. https://learntocodewith.me/programming /python/python-2-vs-python-3.

Fincher, Jon. "Python IDEs and Code Editors (Guide)." Real Python, March 13, 2018. https://realpython .com/python-ides-code-editors-guide.

FreeCodeCamp.org. "Learn Python: Full Course for Beginners." YouTube, July 11, 2018. https://www .youtube.com/watch?v=rfscVS0vtbw.

Programiz.com. "Python Programming Examples. Python by Programiz." Retrieved February 1, 2019. https://www.programiz.com/python-programming /examples.

Python.org. "Python for Beginners." Python.org. Retrieved February 1, 2019. https://www.python .org/about/gettingstarted.

Python for Beginners. "Code Snippets." Python for Beginners. Retrieved February 1, 2019. https://www .pythonforbeginners.com/code-snippets -source-code.

Saeed, Ahsen. "Here Are the Ten Best Programming Languages to Learn in 2019." Coding Infinite, December 22, 2108. https://codinginfinite.com /best-programming-languages-to-learn-2019.

Index

About the Author

Cathleen Small is the author of numerous nonfiction books for children and teens. Before turning to writing, Small edited software, programming, and IT books for a technical publisher. When she is not writing, Small enjoys traveling with her husband and two sons, as well as hanging out with her trusty pug and four mischievous cats.

Photo Credits

Cover © iStockphoto.com/ijeab; cover, p. 1 (code) © iStockphoto.com/scanrail; p. 5 REDPIXEL.PL /Shutterstock.com; p. 6 Artseen/Shutterstock.com; p. 7 Sharaf Maksumov/Shutterstock.com; p. 47 kikujungboy/Shutterstock.com; p. 50 360b /Shutterstock.com; p. 52 izusek/iStock/Getty Images; interior pages border design © iStockphoto.com /Akrain.

Design: Matt Cauli; Editor: Siyavush Saidian; Photo Photo Researcher: Sherri Jackson